MUSIC PUBLISHING OUTLOUD

IN ASSOCIATION WITH ⊛ YAMAHA

The Music Industry Made Crystal Clear

CHRIS BRADFORD

ILLUSTRATIONS BY PAT WEEDON

Head Honcho

Rakesh Sanghvi - Sony-BMG

Whether you're a songwriter, an artist or planning any sort of career in music, a clear understanding of music publishing is vital to your success.

From its origins in printed music, music publishing has evolved into an exciting, creative business which, today, provides much of the framework for the wider music industry.

Songwriting and music publishing underlie so many aspects of our daily entertainment, from records to the use of songs in films, adverts, games and even mobile ringtones. The advent of digitised music has altered the landscape still further, and new opportunities for songwriters and music publishers arise daily.

There is no shortage of songwriting talent in the world and I have been lucky enough to work with some of the best.

For any songwriter today, a working knowledge of publishing deals and the ways in which songs can generate cash, is as important as choosing the right music publisher to represent them.

Whatever the ups and downs and future developments of the music industry may be, I have a feeling that almost every aspect of it will still start with a song...

Rakesh Sanghvi

Rakesh Sanghvi is Managing Director of Sony/ATV Music Publishing (UK) Limited. He joined the company in 1997 having previously worked as an entertainment lawyer in the film and computer games industries. He is also a board member of MCPS.

Disclaimer: This foreword is the personal opinion of Rakesh Sanghvi and not of his employer Sony-BMG.

Hi, I'm Ebony. I'm a performer and songwriter and, just like you, I'm working hard to get myself a record deal. The thing is, I always believed that signing the record deal was the most important goal for an artist. But that's not true…

Writing songs and getting a publishing deal are equally important and will in fact make you more money than signing a record deal!

But what is 'publishing'? How is it different to a record deal? And how can it help you as an artist or songwriter? These are questions that I will help answer for you.

You see, *OutLoud* is your speed-read to the key facts on music publishing. In under 60 pages, we will cover everything you need to know, including what a publisher does, how a song earns money, what different types of publishing contract there are and how a publisher can even help you get a record deal!

Each page will answer an important question related to music publishing. I will then explain each answer further and give you some

Armed with this knowledge, you will understand the importance of music publishing to your career, be able to find the best publisher for your music and sign the most beneficial contract for you!

"In fact, having the right publishing contract can mean the difference between retiring to an elegant mansion on the French Riviera or a small beach hut in Skegness!"

Ebony

What Does A Music Publisher Do?

A music publisher seeks talented songwriters and songs to represent, and, in the same way a record company exploits (i.e. uses or sells) recordings, a music publisher exploits songs in order to earn money for their writers.

Ebony says...

"Understanding the difference between a record company and a publishing company is crucial. Whereas a record company handles the *recordings* of songs, a publisher deals with the *songs* themselves. The publisher is of equal importance to a songwriter as the record company is to an artist."

Ebony advises...

"A music publisher provides a number of different services. Whilst you can do many yourself (known as 'self-publishing'), if you are serious about being a songwriter or performer-writer there are several benefits to having a publisher."

Why Do You Need A Publisher?

A publisher can help a songwriter in five main ways. A publisher can:

- **Collect** money earned by your songs from various music collection societies around the world, as well as register your songs with each of them.
- **Promote** your songs to recording artists, film companies, computer game manufacturers, and so on, and agree a fee for their use.
- **Develop** your songwriting career by organising writing sessions with other writers, providing advice and promoting you to the industry.
- **Fund** you with 'advances' of money – in addition to any provided by a record company – and pay for studio time or equipment to record demos.
- **Protect** your songs by checking they are used only by permission.

Ebony says...

"In return for these services, you 'assign' (i.e. give) the publisher the 'copyright' to your songs for a set amount of time, during which they will take an agreed percentage ('royalty') of any money earned by those songs."

Ebony advises...

"Not all these services will or can be provided by every publisher, so make sure you find out in advance what services they can offer."

What Does Copyright Mean?

Owning or controlling the copyright in a song means you have the right to stop somebody else copying your song whether this is as a recording, a live performance or a written manuscript. You can prevent anyone making changes to your song lyrically or musically. You also have the right to make people pay for copying or using your song.

Ebony says...

"These 'rights' are part of UK law and mean you can make a living as a songwriter. Every time your song is used in a recording, film or TV broadcast, or live performance, you receive a payment (royalty). These royalties are collected by collection societies, like the PRS (Performing Right Society), who then send this money onto you and your publisher."

Ebony advises...

"The ownership of the copyright in a song can be bought or sold by different people, and this is the principle upon which music publishing functions. Owning the copyright, therefore, is very important, since whoever controls the copyright in a song can earn money from it."

What Types Of Publisher Are There?

There are major and independent publishers. A major provides all its services 'in-house', has offices in different countries and is owned by a multi-national corporation, such as Sony-BMG. An independent is smaller, privately owned and often based in one country. Depending on its size, an independent may use other companies for some of its publishing services.

Ebony says...

"In theory, a major should have greater influence and more connections within the music industry to get your songs 'covered' (i.e. recorded) by an artist. However, because they look after so many writers, your songs may get ignored. An independent, whilst possibly having access to fewer opportunities, will be able to offer more individual attention to a writer."

Ebony advises...

"Beware of advertisements offering to publish your song for a fee. A professional publisher will never charge you to sign you or your songs with them."

How Do You Get A Publisher?

If you are signed to a record deal, or about to be, you will probably have several publishers chasing you. If you are not that lucky, then you will have to attract the interest of one yourself. In order to do this, you need to approach a publisher in much the same way you would a record company – with a demo CD.

Ebony says...

"The demo – containing your three best songs – needs to be the highest recording quality you can afford and presented in a professional-looking package with a typed lyric sheet. Ensure that your contact details are on absolutely everything."

Ebony advises...

"If you can, meet and present your demo to the publisher in person. As with any business, it is all about 'who you know'. So take the time to 'network' within the music business and build a good relationship with a publisher first."

Which Publisher Do You Choose?

If you are already signed to a record deal, an important consideration in your choice will be the best financial deal on offer – both in terms of the advance and the royalty split. However, if you are not signed, or are purely a songwriter, then you need to give greater emphasis to the publisher's ability to: i) get artists to record your songs; ii) obtain TV and film commissions; iii) introduce you to the right people to get you a record deal!

Ebony says...

"As a general rule, do not sign a publishing contract with the same company you signed your record deal with. It can occasionally cause problems if you do – for instance, the company may use money earned from your songs to pay off debts created by your record deal. This is known as 'cross-collateralisation'."

Ebony advises...

"It is important that you check the publishing company is well-established and knows what it is doing. Before signing any contract, ask around and find out if the company has a good reputation."

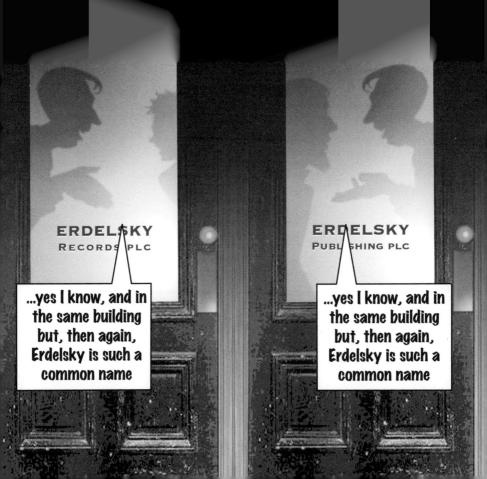

What Is A Publishing Contract?

A publishing contract is the legal agreement between you (the songwriter) and a publishing company. Its main purpose is to give the publisher the rights to exploit your songs. It may be for one song only, a catalogue of songs, or for a set number of songs that you agree to write in the future. These three types of contract are: i) Single Song Assignment (SSA); ii) Exclusive Songwriter Agreement (ESA); iii) Administration Agreement.

Ebony says...

"An SSA is for one song only so leaves you free to sign publishing contracts for other songs – either with the same or a different publisher. An ESA covers all the songs you write during the agreed period of the contract. An Administration Agreement is like an ESA, but the publisher only has to register your songs and collect the money."

Ebony advises...

"This last type offers no advance money, but as the publisher is doing less, you get a bigger share of any income. This is ideal for writers who don't need money upfront or do not want the administrative workload of self-publishing."

What Is In A Publishing Contract?

A contract's main points are: the royalties (what the split is of any money you receive); the advance (how much money you will be given); the term (how long it lasts for); the territory (what countries it applies to); the minimum commitment (what you have to do as the writer); and the retention period (what happens when the contract finishes).

Ebony says...

"The most important part of a publishing contract to the writer is the royalty split offered – even more than the advance or length of term – since this is the element that will dictate how much money you will earn in the long run."

Ebony advises...

"All contracts are negotiable. Decide which element is most important to you (i.e. the advance or royalty) and use the other points to bargain for what you really want."

What Is The Royalty Split?

If you are a pure songwriter, you will get a royalty of between 50% and 75% of the money earned by your songs depending upon the size of advance offered. If you are signed to a record deal, you can expect a more favourable rate of 70-80%. If you are signing an Administration Agreement with a publisher, then it may be nearer 85-90%.

Ebony says...

"A publisher may try to agree a reduced royalty rate for cover recordings because of the 'extra' work involved. This should be avoided, since it is really their job to exploit your songs and many 'covers' come by request of the artists themselves."

Ebony advises...

"At the very minimum, ensure that this reduced rate (usually 50%) applies only to covers obtained as a direct result of their efforts. If you are a pure songwriter, then this clause should be taken out of the contract otherwise you will always get this reduced rate."

What Size Of Advance Can You Get?

A publisher gives you an advance of money to give you the financial freedom to concentrate on your career as a songwriter. The amount can range from a few pounds to tens of thousands of pounds, depending upon how talented the publisher thinks you are, whether or not you have a record deal, what you need to develop your career (e.g. studio time, collaborations, etc) and how much money you may already have earned from your songs.

Ebony says...

"An advance is given to you on the basis that you will pay it back using your royalties. This means that until all the advance is paid off, you will not receive any royalties."

Ebony advises...

"The good news is that the advance is non-returnable. So even if your songs never make any money, you won't have to pay back the advance at the end of the contract period."

When Will You Get The Advance?

If you are purely a songwriter, you may get the entire amount on signing the contract. However, a publisher may want to reduce their financial risk by giving it to you in smaller amounts. If you are an artist, this may work out as 25% on signing the publishing contract, 25% on starting recording and the final half upon release of an album.

Ebony says...

"If, at the end of the first contract period, the pubisher decides to continue representing your songs, you should be paid a further advance. The amount you receive will often be based on a 'min-max' formula – this will be a multiple of what your songs earned the first year, but controlled by a 'minimum' (half) and a 'maximum' (twice) limit based on the value of your first advance."

Ebony advises...

"An alternative to this is the 'rolling advance' whereby every time your royalties pay back your advance, you automatically get given another advance of a similar value. This is useful as royalties can take years to reach your publisher."

How Long Does The Contract Last For?

Most publishing contracts last for a period of one year, with two or three options for the publisher to extend it by a further year each time. The total is known as the term. Each time an option is taken up by the publisher, you will usually get another advance of money.

Ebony says...

"A publishing 'year' lasts for 12 months or until you have had a certain number of songs released on record (depending on the minimum commitment set down in the contract). This is so that a publisher can realistically make back its investment."

Ebony advises...

"In theory, if you never released a record, this would mean you would be signed to the publisher forever! That is why it is crucial your contract states that each option period can only last two or three years. This still means a standard publishing contract with three options could last up to 12 years – a good reason why you should only agree to a maximum of three options."

What Is The Territory?

The territory in most contracts is defined as 'the world'. This is so that the publisher can make money from the use of your songs in every country. For those countries (or territories) that a publisher does not have a direct presence in, they will arrange to have a sub-publisher.

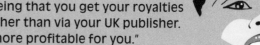

Ebony says...

"You can sign individual contracts with different publishers in each territory, the advantage being that you get your royalties directly from each publisher rather than via your UK publisher. This can work out quicker and more profitable for you."

Ebony advises...

"However, territory-by-territory deals are not popular because they cost more to set-up, require more work and you can get an equal (or higher) advance for signing away the world to one publisher than you may get through signing several different territory deals."

What Is A Sub-Publisher?

A sub-publisher represents the songs of another publisher in a different country. They will register the other publisher's songs in their own country, promote those songs and collect any payment due before sending it onto the original publisher. In return for these services, the sub-publisher usually takes between 15-25% of the total money made by these songs.

Ebony says...

"It can take up to two years to receive any money earned in a foreign country, since there are so many 'middle men' – record companies, radio, TV, local collection societies – who are handling the money."

Ebony advises...

"A publisher does not need to have a sub-publisher. They can join the foreign collection societies directly, but this means there is no-one in that particular territory to promote your songs, chase any earnings or handle the problems of registering your songs in a foreign language."

What Do You Agree To Do?

In return for the advance, a publisher will expect a minimum commitment from you. This will be an agreed number of your songs either released on record by an established record company, or, if you are a pure songwriter, presented on a demo CD to a professional standard.

Ebony says...

"For a recording artist such as a singer–songwriter who co-writes all their songs, the minimum commitment may be 50% of a 10 track album."

Ebony advises...

"It is important that any minimum commitment you agree to is realistic and achievable. If you write or release less than agreed, then your advance for that option period will be reduced accordingly, and under these circumstances you may have to pay some of it back."

What's A Synchronisation Fee?

If someone wants to use your song in a film, commercial or advert, a publisher will allow them to use (i.e. 'license') that song in return for a fee. This is known as a 'synchronisation fee'. The amount entirely depends upon the popularity of the song in question.

Ebony says...

"This fee can range from £10-20,000 for a major film, and from £30,000 to upwards of £1 million for a hit song in a commercial. The fee is entirely negotiable dependent upon the popularity of the song in question, but it is in addition to any 'performance' royalties you may get."

Ebony advises...

"A publisher will want a bigger royalty share for getting a synchronisation deal, since there is a lot of work involved, and many film and TV prospects come to nothing despite the hard work. It is important, however, that this bigger share only applies to deals that they directly found for you."

What Happens When The Contract Ends?

After the end of your contract, the publisher continues to represent your songs for a set period of time. This is known as the 'retention period' and can last an additional 10 to 20 years after the term ends. During this time, the publisher continues to earn their share of the money from these songs for the work and investment they put into your career.

Ebony says...

"The retention period tends to apply only to songs recorded and released during the contract period. Generally, any songs that you wrote and were not used by you or any other artist during this time return to you, free of any obligation to the publisher one or two years after the term has finished."

Ebony advises...

"Do not sign a retention period for life of copyright (although with library music and specifically commissioned music this is more normal). The maximum should be 20 years and if you agree to this, you may be able to get a better royalty rate or even another advance halfway through the retention period."

Can I Publish My Own Songs?

Yes. You do not need to have a publisher. It is possible to manage, promote and collect the money your songs earn by yourself. This is known as 'self-publishing' or 'self-administration'. To do this, you have to join the music collection societies directly and register your songs with them.

Ebony says...

"The benefits of this are: i) you keep the copyright to your songs; ii) you get your money quicker; iii) you don't split your earnings with a publisher. The disadvantages are: i) the large amount of admin work required; ii) the lack of money in advance; iii) loss of income from non-collected royalties in foreign territories; iv) there is only you to promote your songs."

Ebony advises...

"Due to the difficulties of this option, usually only successful writers with a good track record, or a writer who can afford to hire an administrator, would normally consider self-publishing."

So What's A Good Publishing Deal?

Generally most songwriters, whether signed to a record deal or not, can negotiate:

- Term of one year plus two options
- Minimum commitment of 10 tracks co-written per year
- Retention period of 15 years

Ebony says...

"A typical advance for a writer who is not signed to a record deal would be between £10-20,000 for the first year; whilst a signed writer could be looking at several times that amount to start with."

Ebony advises...

"Remember the royalty share is possibly the most important factor in a publishing contract and you need to be aiming for a 75/25 split. This is often achievable by agreeing to a lower initial advance."

Music Publishing Companies

Ebony says...

"One of the best resources for finding a music publisher is the Music Publishers' Association (www.mpaonline.org.uk), who provide an online listing of their member publishers. For a full listing of all UK publishers, though, you will need a copy of the annual *Music Week Directory* (www.musicweek.co.uk)."

Major music publishers include:

- EMI Music Publishing (www.emimusicpub.com)
- Sony-BMG Music Publishing (www.sonybmg.com)
- Universal Music Publishing (www.universalmusicpublishing.com)

Independent music publishers include:

- Chrysalis Music Publishing (www.chrysalismusic.co.uk)
- Independent Music Group (www.independentmusicgroup.com)
- Peer Music Publishing (www.peermusic.com)

British Academy Of Composers & Songwriters

The British Academy Of Composers & Songwriters is the largest composer/songwriter membership organisation in the world, representing the interests of over 3,000 UK writers and composers. It numbers Britain's leading songwriters amongst its members and honours the best of them at the annual Ivor Novello Awards.

Ebony says...

"One of the most useful services The Academy offers is its writing and business workshops designed to help develop new talent. The Academy is also able to offer advice on contracts and agreements."

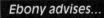

Ebony advises...

"If you are serious about becoming a songwriter, then you should consider joining the British Academy Of Composers & Songwriters."

For further information, call The Academy on +44 (0)20 7636 2929 or visit their website: www.britishacademy.com

Useful Music Industry Organisations

Ebony says...

"There are a number of music industry organisations that deal with music publishing, and you may wish to contact them for further information. These include..."

- **MPA (Music Publishers Association)** – represents the interests of UK music publishers to the Government, music industry, media and public. Website: www.mpaonline.org.uk
- **PRS (Performing Right Society)** – is a membership organisation of composers, songwriters, authors and publishers of music of all styles (including classical, pop, jazz and music for films, adverts and TV) whose main function is to collect and distribute music royalties on behalf of its writer members. Website: www.mcps-prs-alliance.co.uk
- **MCPS (Mechanical-Copyright Protection Society)** – is the UK collection society that collects, administers and distributes mechanical royalties (i.e. money generated from the recording of music on various formats such as CD and MP3). The MCPS then distributes this income to writer and publisher members. Website: www.mcps-prs-alliance.co.uk

Further Reading

"If, after reading this book, you wish to learn more about music publishing and the music business, then I can recommend the following books..."

- *How To Succeed In The Music Business* by Allan Dann & John Underwood (Omnibus Press)
- *Heart & Soul: Revealing The Craft Of Songwriting* by Chris Bradford (Sanctuary Publishing)
- *All You Need to Know Abut The Music Business* by Donald Passman (Penguin Books)

Other books in the OutLoud series include:

- *Record Deals OutLoud* (SMT)
- *Artist Management OutLoud* (SMT)

For serious musicians, songwriters and producers the world over, Yamaha musical instruments and music technology have become synonymous with quality and creativity. Yamaha plays an important role in the creative and recording process and our development people pay close attention to the current and future needs of musicians everywhere.

We are proud of our supportive relationships with emerging and established talent, and hope that this exciting OUTLOUD series will assist all those seeking an audience to better navigate the nuances and complexities of the music business good luck!

Keep writing and keep playing - if you've got it they want it!

For more information on Yamaha instruments, equipment and music support schemes please visit www.yamaha-music.co.uk

YAMAHA

ESSENTIAL TOOLS

Published by **SMT**
an imprint of Bobcat Books Limited
8/9 Frith Street, London W1D 3JB, UK.

Exclusive Distributors:
Music Sales Limited
Distribution Centre, Newmarket Road, Bury St Edmunds, Suffolk IP33 3YB, UK.

Music Sales Corporation
257 Park Avenue South, New York, NY10010, USA.

Music Sales Pty Limited
120 Rothschild Avenue, Rosebery, NSW 2018, Australia.

Order No. SMT2244
ISBN 1-84609-531-X
This book © Copyright 2006 Bobcat Books Limited,
a division of Music Sales Limited.

Printed in the EU

Your Guarantee of Quality
As publishers, we strive to produce every book to the highest commercial standards. Throughout, the printing and binding have been planned to ensure a sturdy, attractive publication which should give years of enjoyment. If your copy fails to meet our high standards, please inform us and we will gladly replace it.

www.musicsales.com

DH

070.
579
4
BRA